I SPY

CHRISTMAS

THIS BOOK BELONGS TO

I Spy with my little eye someting beginning with ...

A is for ...

Angel

I Spy with my little eye someting beginning with ...

B is for ...

Bell

I Spy with my little eye someting beginning with ...

C is for ...

candy cane

I Spy with my little eye someting beginning with ...

C is for ...

Candle

I Spy with my little eye someting beginning with ...

D is for ...

Doll

I Spy with my little eye someting beginning with ...

E is for ...

Elf

I Spy with my little eye someting beginning with ...

F is for ...

Fireplace

I Spy with my little eye someting beginning with ...

G is for ...

Gift

I Spy with my little eye someting beginning with ...

G is for ...

Gingerbread man

I Spy with my little eye someting beginning with ...

H is for ...

Holly

I Spy with my little eye someting beginning with ...

H is for ...

Hot Chocolate

I Spy with my little eye someting beginning with ...

J is for ...

Jingle

I Spy with my little eye someting beginning with ...

L is for ...

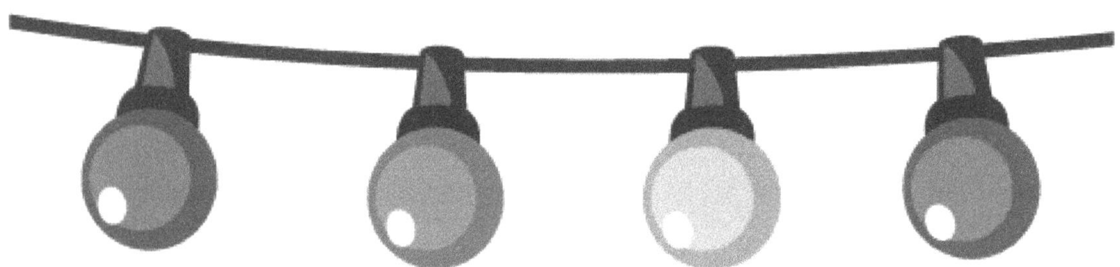

Lights

I Spy with my little eye someting beginning with ...

M is for ...

Mistletoe

I Spy with my little eye someting beginning with ...

P is for ...

Pudding

I Spy with my little eye someting beginning with ...

P is for ...

Penguin

I Spy with my little eye someting beginning with ...

Q is for ...

Quince

I Spy with my little eye someting beginning with ...

R is for ...

Reindeer

I Spy with my little eye someting beginning with ...

S is for ...

Sock

I Spy with my little eye someting beginning with ...

S is for ...

Santa Claus

I Spy with my little eye someting beginning with ...

T is for ...

Christmas Tree

I Spy with my little eye someting beginning with ...

V is for ...

Vixen

I Spy with my little eye someting beginning with ...

W is for ...

Wreath